A QUIET GATHERING

David Scott

A QUIET GATHERING

with drawings by Graham Arnold

BLOODAXE BOOKS

ISBN: 0 906427 68 1

First published 1984 by
Bloodaxe Books Ltd,
P.O. Box 1SN,
Newcastle upon Tyne NE99 1SN.

Bloodaxe Books Ltd acknowledges
the financial assistance of Northern Arts.

Typesetting by
Tyneside Free Press Workshop Ltd, Newcastle upon Tyne.

Printed in Great Britain by
Unwin Brothers Ltd, Old Woking, Surrey.

For Miggy,
Adam & Lucy

Acknowledgements

Acknowledgements are due to the editors of the following publications in which some of these poems have appeared: *Adam's Dream* (Cumbria Literature, 1981), *The Franciscan, Grand Piano, Iron, New Fire, Poetry Review, St Alban's Abbey News, Sunday Times* and *The Times Literary Supplement.* Some also appeared in two pamphlets, *Thorn and Flower* (Dodman Press, 1976) and *Days Out* (Mandeville Press, 1978); 'The Presbytery Cellar' was published by Starwheel Press, and 'Bishop Taylor's Remedies against Tediousness of Spirit' by the Derwent Press.

'Groundsmen', 'Leavesden Asylum, 1880', 'Letters from Baron Von Hügel to a Niece', 'Scale Model', 'Scattering Ashes' and 'Queen's Park, Glasgow' were broadcast on *Poetry Now* (BBC Radio 3). 'Kirkwall Auction Mart' and 'On Visiting Keats House' were broadcast on BBC-2 television.

'Kirkwall Auction Mart' won first prize in the 1978 *Sunday Times*/BBC national poetry competition.

Contents

Kirkwall Auction Mart

There are no bolts that do not exactly
fit the gates into and out of the store-ring.
Hundreds of times a day the same slamming iron
marshals cattle lots, hooves fighting the sand,
until the stick smacks them into view.
A nod decides the hidden bidders
and for these ghosts a litany is sung
bridging the jump in bids by the ancient
rattling of tongues until a bashed hand settles it.
Paper slips locate the buyers. We might
have guessed it would be a man of dull cloth,
hunched over the front rail, his smoke
joining the wreath of snorted breath high up
in the roof, who knew his business, and bought.

Illness

Hers was the vacant seat by the door.
To choose the nearest was her way of coping
with the recent bother of always feeling tired,
especially today, with the sudden change in weather.
At first, the shopping basket held her up,
but sleep soon capsized her
to the angle a holed tanker is towed at.
I wondered if the illness would come as a surprise
to her, leaving the family to shop for muddled meals;
and how she would wake up eventually;
by a kindly tap at the end of the line,
or in panic, not sure of the stop.

Leavesden Asylum, 1880

All the apparatus is well made.
The deathcart for example has its canvas
tight on the wood, and the wheels turn straight.
Even the certificates are stylishly printed
on fine paper fit for the Master's signature.
The rules are numbered and in bold print,
defining the length of visits, and formalising
a whole range of separations; stamping out
the illicit gift pressed into the palm
before the hour when the gate is locked
and the authorities will not be roused.
The architects had as many bricks as they required,
and since none would admire it, the blocks
could use up the sky, with each ward
the precise dimension of all the others.
The window sills are high enough to hold up
a face vacant as bread for a hand to wave at
from the yard. February is cold except
for a bed's length from the stove. August,
too hot for a canvas dress and black, lace-up boots.

Venus

Behind a counter, she was offering silks
and bells in the perfumed air.
Each mirror had its own angle
came up with its own tender zone
of elbow, press of the crown of hair,
tilting foot, nape of neck.
I could see why she was chosen
for Venus. It was summer
when all sorts of things can happen.
Let her be Venus for a while,
until the first hard winter
rings the bell of the boutique behind her.

Letters from Baron Von Hügel to a Niece

His day was not really complete until
he sealed with a gentle middle finger
a letter to his niece, heralding the arrival
of books. It smelt of camphor. The advice
was a comfort to her: 'Give up Evensong,
and even if dying never strain.'
It was surprising counsel from one so scrupulous;
whose sharp pencil noted on both margins of a page,
and hovered, like a teacher's, over spelling.
Walking into Kensington with the letter,
his muffler tight against the frost,
he reassures himself that directing a soul
is not only a matter of angel's talk, it is
also the knack of catching the evening post.

For John Ball

Travelling from Durham on the early train
we would arrive without warning, and in no time,
you half into your cassock, there would be coffee.
If there was no reply, then either you were tired
of passing traffic; or were saying mass in church,
which was reached from the square with the plane trees
through a parish of tenements and seedy hotels.
Your other parish was us. We came to you
because like your favourite poet Stevie Smith
you sat still; and had a private voice
which only carried as far as it needed.
News of your death came as no surprise.
I sensed that one day I would turn up
and you would not be able to rise, tiny priest,
on the one, strong, slender hand that did for two.

Queen's Park, Glasgow

They came separately hoping for a game
but passing the all-weather tennis court
sagging with pools of rain, it did not look hopeful.
The man in the pitch-and-put cabin
looked dismally out at the two lads
knocking wild balls at the last tin flag.
Soon he could go home. The bowlers put on
their brogues, as charms against the rain,
but one, not doing up his laces under the flap
knew it was no good, and nipping his cigarette,
said so. It was enough. The single file trailed round
the cinder path, macs covering blazers heavy
with the club badge; woods still snug with the jack.

Groundsmen

The pile of cuttings puts on dreadful weight,
swelters in the season, and leaks treacle.
Beside it, the tractor and the cutters drip oil
into the earth floor, in a shed where cobwebs
link the roof to the wired window and the oil drums.
The twisted blades and the spiked roller
rest from the nibbling and pricking of the pitch;
and in the corner a white liner, clogged white
round the wheels, darkens towards the handles.
The quiet men whose stuff this is
have the next shed along. Their door shuts
neatly to, unlike the tractor shed
where the door drags and billows against the bricks.
It was a secret kingdom for a boy.
I envied them their work; lending out bats,
lowering the posts, the twirl of the cutter
at the end of a straight run; and their shed
at the edge of the known world.

Flower Rota

The niche in the pillar
with its chance ledge
had been chosen
by two mothers jointly
for sons killed in action.

On Saturday, in memory
of the day their sons fell,
they arrange the flowers;
brush the fallen petals;
return the watering can
to the tap by the wall.

Early on the Sunday morning
they can see the solidago
shot with sun, atoning
for their death on the hill
that terrible April.

A Long Way from Bread

1.

We have come so far from bread.
Rarely do we hear the clatter of the mill wheel;
see the flour in every cranny,
the shaking down of the sack, the chalk on the door,
the rats, the race, the pool,
baking day, and the old loaves:
cob, cottage, plaited, brick.

We have come so far from bread.
Once the crock said 'bread'
and the bread was what was there,
and the family's arm went deeper down each day
to find it, and the crust was favoured.

We have come so far from bread.
Terrifying is the breach between wheat and table,
wheat and bread, bread and what goes for bread.
Loaves come now in regiments, so that loaf
is not the word. *Hlaf*
is one of the oldest words we have.

2.

I go on about bread
because it was to bread
that Jesus trusted
the meaning he had of himself.
It was an honour for bread
to be the knot in the Lord's handkerchief
reminding him about himself. So,
O bread, breakable;
O bread, given;
O bread, a blessing;
count yourself lucky, bread.

3.

Not that I am against wafers,
especially the ones produced under steam
from some hidden nunnery
with our Lord crucified into them.
They are at least unleavened, and fit the hand,
without remainder, but it is still
a long way from bread.
Better for each household to have its own bread,
daily, enough and to spare,
dough the size of a rolled towel,
for feeding angels unawares.
Then if the bread is holy,
all that has to do with bread is holy:
board, knife, cupboard,
so that the gap between all things is closed
in our attention to the bread of the day.

4.

I know that
'man cannot live on bread alone'.
I say, let us get the bread right.

Poplar

At the heart
of the trembling poplar
is a leaf stalk, ribbed
and longer than the stalk itself
which is how the wind
can whisper its rumour
right across Lombardy.

The lopped trunks
spindle thin
like foals' legs
hold their scanning leaves
crisp as radar
decoding the sun.

The wood of the ash tree
is used for matches, cart floors,
and around Jerusalem and Galilee
for crosses; which is why
the blood silver coppice
still shivers in remembrance.

Ash

The clumps of winter seeds
hang off the branch
like warders' keys;
those branches which
have ashed urchins.

The tough, close-grained wood
made shafts for spears.
At the Battle of Maldon
ash meant spear.

Take a leaf
and close it like a book;
being pinnate
it will couple perfectly.

I know it best
for the charcoal buds,
and the stick that won't snap;
only fracture, shred
with the twist, and hang limp.

Mud

The books call it
rich, friable loam,
but me and my son
say mud. See it hold the stream
like a farmer's palm.
Air gets at the iron
oxidising. All the same
we see rust
encouraging the frozen flame.
Take cold fistfuls,
like woad;
paint it on—
see how the hairs spring gold.

Canal

The canal is asleep with history.
It has eaten too much, and is stuck
between cemented locks. Its maw
packed with pram; bicycle frame;
tyres; springs; cooker; sun.
It has the quietness of courtyards.
Swans sleep the sun away: their
snouts in the pits of their wings.
The stained glass tremors
on the belly of the hump-back.

Jet

Her wrist had turned to dust:
become taste of must in the cave;
but her bracelet
slept through civilisations
sealed under stalagmite.
It is jet
and black as a calf's eye.

Up the Dale they call jet
candle-coal. They say,
'it's packed so tight
time can't get a finger in it.'

For Martin

Strange how gorse
has thorn and rich flower
both—all along
the hills and roadsides
from Carrowkeel to Portsalon
and on the slopes of Murren.

My Saviour caught his coat
on gorse. Fingering
the torn cloth and trammelled thread
he spoke of death being
thorn and rich flower,
both.

Midland Red

1.

The tin sign tells us
they still sell Lion Tea
at the corner shop.
Gobstoppers
drop out for a penny
from full dispensers.
Stores sell back-studs
from miniature sets of drawers.
Everywhere, privet,
which short cuts to the ice-cream van
have rubbed bare.

2.

Thanks to Littlewoods
a thousand Doreens
catch their fingernails
in their Mix 'n' Match
Nylon frilled pillow-cases.

In the Berni Inn Rogues Bar
we get curly butter,
and say,
'How about rosé?'

3.

The pensioner with his pass
as creased as his trouser crotch
revolves his tea-stained dentures
and calls the driver, 'Driver!'

The colour of the washing
is mainly pink,
blown up like a wind-sock
over the dahlias.
Red and black for Ansells.
Fire and coal.
Lipstick and cinders.

Winston Churchill

On the morning of the funeral,
when the cranes were practising their salute,
the Myth woke up to his last responsibility.
He elbowed his way into his braces,
each shoulder some sort of clinched strategy,
and the trousers settled like theatre curtains
over the last generation of shiny shoes.

The responsibility lay around
our semi in the form of symbols
just a bit too big to manage:
the British Warm that gave me aircraft-carrier
shoulders; five inches of measly bath water;
and a rhetoric, which my father could turn on
for the small fee of being believed.

New College Dining Hall

The stampede went that way,
and it's sabbath again.
The benches breathe out,
while up there a ruff
goffered like a paper dart
in a rectangle of varnish
semaphores to the last Warden.
He is casual: legs crossed, grey suit,
hush-puppies. I sense that
eating is just a fraction
of the mute affair.
The rest is high old air:
spiralling, mote-filled.

Dusk at Lough Derryduff

The evening opened out like that.
We gradually put on silhouettes
like pullovers, and joined the march
of rushes, carrying their panicles

across the sky. Gumboots thudded the turf,
leaping the bog.
The parents way behind,
sounding as if along with us.

We got to the cars first,
and sat with the rods and the picnic case,
on the verge, willing the cloud
to cover the moon's bright face.

The keys came last.
The boot was stuffed. The dog, stowed.
We heaved each other's boots off;
saw liquid lights tremble in deep crofts.

Driving home, the simple line of hills
made finger-tracing
easy on the windows, still
thick with condensation from the dog's breathing.

Beeleigh Abbey

That particular prime
when the corncrake and the scent
of the goldflower met in the air,
the monks chose the Blackwater.
White habits worked the marsh: settled
like gulls on a burnt field.

But the monks are gone now,
and their prayer is aorist too.
Perhaps the tide stole it away
for salt: gathered it
on the sunken ribcage of the ferry.

The Seamen's Reading Room, Southwold

Cricket pavilions are like this:
photos crowding the walls; outdoor furniture
inside; the same uneven floor.
Instead of teams, here are skippers,
their oil-skins fading from sepia to jaundice,
their pin-eyes daring the horizon.

Back at the clubhouse, one
stands up to deal, sits, fans his hand,
throws a casual card, with all his arthritis
moves a heavy match along.
He remembers when the tide was trumps,
or the gale; long before this foursome
became a model of itself.
The one in the corner fingers
his newspaper like a net.

The Book of Common Prayer 1549

This is just what you might expect
a Prayer Book to be like. This is
what we always thought about rain;
about dying, and marriage, and God.
We needed only the help which
the right placing of a relative pronoun
could manage. Words, then, said what they meant;
they bit. A man was a houseband
until death departed him.
And all was for common use:
printed in Fleet Street,
at the sign of the sun,
over against the conduit.

On Visiting Keats House

I had anticipated the wall-to-wall
carpet; the bookstall; and the staff toilet;
but not the brown ink of Keats's handwriting:
neat, round, and vertical.
Our duffle coats, when we leaned
on the glass to read this letter to Fanny,
gave a slight tap of toggle. We read,
with eyes only, a postscript full of dashes
and torment. I recalled the ring
he sent her, which she hid under a thin glove.
We replaced the cover, bought cards,
and left: aware that even one's frustration
from now, would be an imitation.
That if we were brave enough to say what we felt
this winter, it would have been said before,
in ink the colour of tea, to perfection.

Early Communion

Checking times the day before by brushing
blown snow off a leaning board, I guessed
that eight o'clock would chime
on a handful of us, and the priest.
The service was according to the book,
the only variables being
my random fist of coins scooped into a bag
and the winter jasmine above the holy table.
For the rest, we knelt where it advised us to,
ungainly but meaning it, trusting to the words set
(on paper difficult to separate)
that what we did was acceptable.

After Mass

There is a way of setting down vestments:
chasuble, girdle, stole, alb;
and the amice, which is Christ's blindfold.
Each morning they come orderly off,
before the priest settles back into his belt
and considers breakfast.
A vague prayer at the altar rail
is nailed with the sign of the cross;
and as the trebles in the vestry
hit the sky with a practice scale,
he rises. The mass is done.
Another day is satisfied.

Heveningham Hall, Suffolk

Wandering through someone's planned
view between lake and mansion,
I excite lambs snaffling at dugs,
and lope through small acres of chancy sun.
This is spring and a stately home.
In a decade my half ticket
will be found in Crabbe's Poems,
and the Illustrated Guide
will be uncurled the other way.
Through one long corridor of rooms
I notice silk, shredding beneath
plastic sheets; and mirrors
shrinking in their gilt frames.
The relief of coming out is the door
encouraging the sun to make geometry
out of the stone floor.

A Walk near Fulford Hospital

The wind tugging the couch-grass
and racing the Edinburgh express
across flat, soaked fields
stopped short at the hospital.

There I imagined patients fumbling awake
making mouldy heat out of yesterday's breath;
the sash windows painted into position.
The heat from the cream radiators
paled those who pressed against them;
and the cords, meant to puppet the ventilation,
had long since been pulled completely through.

Grateful for the freedom
to angle into the wind,
I noticed both the ridging on the elm
and the tangled raffia of potato stalks;
the cowl of my coat turning at will
as I walked, in and out of the ruts, home.

Cycling Holiday

They prop up the tandem outside the shop,
exchange toffees, slot cards for the parents
into the wall. The wind is fresh
and tugs at the map where tanned fingers
trace the next stretch: lunch
safe in the panier. The shop bell
rings out a regular customer; and they are set
ready on the pedals. But just a moment
while he scratches his bare knee
and she rearranges her pony tail.

T.E. Lawrence to George Brough

It is the silkiest thing
I have ever ridden,
better than the Triumph in Cairo.
Yours has the spring sprocket
making it so mild at 50.
Stretching the goggles
over the shiny peak; gauntlets
flexed comfortably on, I move the two ends
of this long machine into a single bird
gathering speed through the open barrier
which drops its salute behind me.
We know the flat road into Cambridge;
the changes of gear around Ayot St Lawrence;
the midges on the Surrey switchback.
With my visor down so to speak I charge
at Mr Hardy's country to make it
back to camp before lights-out.
Thank you for the spare plugs.
I only needed one: the other
lasted till I got to Welwyn.
It is a perfect steed.

A Prayer at the putting on of our clothes

By our beds we were given a chair
and on it went the simple clothes of the day.
Each had the same sort
and all were grey.
This was what had to be, until four o'clock
and then 'scruff dress', softer at the edges,
meant baggier trousers, aertex shirt, pullover.
Grey was still the colour. We chanced nothing else
except for the tie which was maroon and dark blue.
Almost grey. This order had its effect.
Now the old changes of clothes are still around
to challenge the new. Why this? Why that?
Is it work or play today? Worse still
we go by the weather and change and change all day.
My prayer is again for the simple grey.

Old English Household Life
by Gertrude Jekyll, 1925

Nostalgia was just browning up
especially with regard to household things
in West Surrey when Gertrude Jekyll wrote.
Museums were typing out the labels
with a black typewriter's huge letters:
dog turnspit, smock, pepper pot.
Even then we were being removed from dirt
and the patient keeping in of lights and fires.
The brasses, no more catching the sun,
came off the sweating foreheads of the horses,
onto the pub wall. Lych-gates no longer
rested the dead on the final walk up the path.
Each chapter heading was an epitaph.

Rain

This is the rain the Brontës knew
knocking at the tomb-chests
like knuckle-bones thrown to dogs.
The drains drink to bursting.
The yews blacken, and the grass
toughens against the stones
ripening against the scythe.
The sisters have exercise books
from which they look up now and then
to watch the rain, in rods, refreshing
the dead, and memories of the dead.

Mist

It was always the same drawing;
a house on a hill
with a path winding to the door
and the sun beating down.
I saw a house the same today
just below the mist, and wondered
how another drawing could say
people live there now?
What could convey the placing of clocks?
Or the weight the seats take between bouts
of work? Or how the overalls
hoisted between hams
take a long time to dry
on days when the damp
gets even into the fire?
A brush stroke would do:
slanting the roof, rubbish by the path
too heavy to move, sheep's wool
hanging vertical from the wire.

Herdwick

Some work the sampler of the moor
their Quaker grey heads
following the text, stitch by stitch.
Others take a journey
at a tinker's pace, their wagon of rags
splashed with ochre, leadening in the rain.
The rest recline, passing the parcel
with their jaws, yet adamant
in their own seat, happy or not to win.

Curlew

The mist deadened the island
but the curlew swerving over the outhouse
was the last to succumb. Its bill
like a tool the sailmaker has to hand
is so turned as to glide in on the worm
in the sand; its cry, sharp as a blade on a strop.
In all this muffled dusk, little,
except a filling burn, and this bird,
beating the bounds of its woollen cage.

Border Ballad

Nothing untoward this morning
as the sun lifts the long-necked
hollyhock back up the garden wall;
and the snail's signature
silvers an unkempt path.
Only later the post arrives
with its heavy crested paper
folded in four, and the flimsy one
from the war. Then we can see
as the evening comes, and from this height,
all ten fingers of rain
press home their curse
into the steel water of the Firth.

Flanking Sheep in Mosedale

All summer the sheep were strewn like crumbs
across the fell, until the bracken turned brittle
and it was time they were gathered
into the green patchwork of closer fields.
Dogs and men sweep a whole hillside in minutes
save for the stray, scared into a scramble
up a gully. A dog is detached: whistled off
by the shepherd who in one hand
holds a pup straining at the baling twine
and in the other, a crook light as a baton.
His call cuts the wind across the tarn:
it is the voice of the first man, who
booted it across this patch to bring
strays to the place where he would have them.
You can tell that here is neither love nor money
but the old game fathers have taught sons to win.
It is done well, when the dogs
lie panting, and the sheep encircled dare not move.

Ruskin's 'Sketches from Nature'

There is a hurry in his sketch. The cloud
will only stay a while like that
before a serious change obliterates.
A cloud will not stay quiet: it burns
and draws in all that is around,
cusping and reeling across the Old Man of Coniston.
On his desk are the practice wads
of cotton, and the books to verify
what a cloud is. He delights to find
that clouds do not grow, but are sculpted down
by the warm air around, like masons
working on Venetian stone. How difficult
to get them down on paper.
So many sacks of flour. Except for Turner
the master of the cloud, who in his vignettes
and storm studies seemed to get them right.

Quodlibet

It would be a good title.
It pleased Duns Scotus
and we share initials.
All those airy questions packed
into the neat hutch of a Latin word;
quodlibet: exactly separating this from that.
It got to such a pitch with him,
and I know how he felt,
that his stomach would not settle
for less than the essence of a thing.
The pleasure of getting it right
meant he could draw the blankets
round his chin, and sleep tight.
The converse I find is true,
tossing this way and that,
sorting out which, if any,
of the possible conditional clauses, will do.

William Nicolson
(1655–1727)

A boy from Plumbland
who took to declensions and tables
till the wax waterfalled and sputtered
has left us his notes
legible, on churches, churchyards,
wild flowers and rare words.

From the concern for detail
I had imagined a saintlier face.
The portrait, leaning out on long strings,
has it ruddy against lawn,
filling out with dinner towards the gilt frame:
one on the stairs at Rose, the other in the Hall at Queens.

He was a born Archdeacon, committed
to journeys and the minute particular;
and caustic, rowing with the Dean
over matters of protocol.
His pocket knife handy
for the constant scraping of lichen
from the thin lines of Norse runes.

Of the generation who wondered
on which day in March the Deluge commenced,
and the exact timing of the Fall;
their accuracy miscalculated God
but produced nice diagrams of the Roman Wall.

It mattered to him that the sanctuary was swept
and how the library at Derry was kept;
and for joy in the summer season, a dozen letters
or so, and rambling, simpling etc.

Dean Tait

(Archibald Tait was Dean of Carlisle. In the space of one month, March 1856, five of his daughters died in an epidemic of scarlet fever.)

Quite put aside were any thoughts
of the state of the Cathedral roof.
Instead, a quiet agony, waiting
for the stethoscope's final figure of eight,
and the click of the doctor's bag.
He never thought there could be this routine
to death: the prayer book, the size of his palm;
his wife, half in doubt because of the fever,
hiding the sick-room drawings away;
and at their prayers each day
in a borrowed house, they tested
the Bible texts against a silent nursery.

David Livingstone on the eve
of discovering the Victoria Falls

The lamp picks out the flint-lock
a page of the Greek text of Luke,
his tin travelling-box, and his cap's red satin
upturned, holding open the note-book
at today's new words: thunder, smoke,
waiting, rainbow. On these nights of clear skies
he is grateful for his warm shirt,
its Scotch wool; at the end of the night,
this noise. The roar draws near.
The roar and the smoke have become familiar,
more thunderous: more like fire than water.
Another day will tell, another night,
what water burns, what fire ignites both rainbows.

The Presbytery Cellar

It was like a potting shed
the warm sea-light falling on the suitcase,
the statues, the thurible hanging on the door knob:
all the brown junk that never made it
back to church. No housekeeper
would dare the steps under the electric wires
looped like bunting; only the priests
annually for the crib, or in search
of the patches and glue to mend a tyre,
went down cautious, smoking, out of breath.
After each half-jammed drawer, a puff
a limp refusal to go on. What use
a rusty soutane button, a veil
yellowing to the colour of sherry.
Again there was no cause
to unpack the copies of the Fathers
sent from the Mother House.

The Burial of Mrs Pusey

The ruffle of crape and silk
moved round the quadrangle, shuffling
black and scarlet, faces alabaster
against the tidy, honey stone
into an unpredictable wind.
Gloved hands could hold veils down
but one thing lay beyond reach.
Doctor Pusey knew that well, but
it had not been so much brought home
as when the pall fluttered
like an uneven breath.
Something in the levity of it
locked for ever over that pavement
his melancholy tread.

Playing in the Yard

His hands seem to say
this toy is quite good
one large plastic ring through five,
colours shocking to the eye,
but it lies now where he threw it.

Ah yes, the gardening boot is better
fitting the whole of him,
a mysterious well
into which he drops his voice.

Better still, the pocket of the pram
feeling for tissues and old biscuits;
until the toy, neon in the grey yard,
flashes its frantic appeal.

Scale Model

I thought the view was familiar.
We made it one Summer Term just like that:
hills, patchwork fields, a river's meander;
and lead sheep permanently at grass.
It was a project for Open Day when we enforced
enclosure acts with a deft cut of foam rubber.
Peasants' cottages leant perilously up against themselves;
while the Manor stood solid in black and white gloss.
The model and the view collided, momentarily; but
the train sped on; and the mirror, which was a pond
slipped off the little world
turned up behind the stock cupboard.

Red Indian

One day, the tomahawk
split my brother's head.
He was General Custer,
and, as I thought, deserved it.
The blood made his hair shine black,
and in the quiet before the howl,
a breeze shivered the crows' feathers
down my bare, Red Indian back.

The Taste of Cast Iron

Some time before the Coronation
the playground was proposed
and seconded; the details
to be worked out later: like
who would pollard the limes
and grease the joints of the swings.
Since when the motor mower's throb
has ebbed and flowed all day
to the edge of the asphalt
and away to the putting green.
A thundery afternoon incubates
a mild nausea on the roundabout.
I can taste iron. From the top of the slide
there are all the roofs and gardens of the estate
the coal bunkers, and bare patches on the lawn.
I taste the iron of fire-escapes and railings,
the bars of bus-stop barriers; gate latches;
and wash them down with one
slide after another.

Roof

The roof is for keeping out rain.
Good Welsh Slate it is
set neat on the lath
overlapping the join beneath.
Not for drying flax this roof,
but angled to survive remarkable weather.
After each lashing I look
to see how the ranks have fared
and notice how they lighten
back in colour to the same purple-green.
There were days when the rain
went straight through, and the slates
got stacked in the long grass.
It was worth knocking it all out
and starting, from the shoulders of the wall, again.

Botanical Gardens

I was settled in this Eden
when he waved from a long way off
indicating it was closing time.
In slow motion I waved consent
and sauntered to the gate
over light shale, between precise edges of grass.
The Latin names came lazily off their signs:
take it or leave it; we are known.
Hoe blades now resting on the soil
shone with use. I slowed right down
for beyond the gate something disturbed the air
more than here: things with no name
or the wrong name; weeds; mud
drying on the spades. There seemed
no carrying out the secret of the place.
It snaked back, like the pipes
in the Glass House, to a hidden tap.

Gwen John

Her cats move freely
about the room, while
dusk thins its colour
down to ash and
less takes over from more.
She has in mind a girl
whose hand rests in its lap
gentle from illness.
A Mother Superior
has the same stillness;
and villagers with comfy hats
settle into their seats in church.
She moves the quiet edges of the world
into line, and places a teapot within reach.

The Oxford Dictionary of Nursery Rhymes

These we let out,
like butterflies from spring window-sills.
They have slept a long time
but rise up from the memory
as we rock from foot to foot,
humming at first, then
our own version of the words,
See-saw, Margery Daw.

We like it in the barn
the beamed roof, the earth floor,
the sun angling through the doorway,
saying nothing, making logs
drop off the sawing horse
as if we had all day,
content with but a penny.

For Brother Jonathan

Brother Jonathan, the guardian of Alnmouth Friary, died
after being washed out to sea on 31 July 1982.)

I remember the water. For a second
let it right over me.
It knocked out my breath
on the first eager morning there
before breakfast. All day
the waves breathed on to the sand and the sea-coal;
and at night, looking from the library
I think a beacon swept them
about the turn of every page.

The quiet and the sea: I thought
this was the life. It wasn't
entirely. You let me into that secret,
Jonathan, gently, and over the years
through the contents of a whole bundle
of brown envelopes said as much.

We met again in Cambridge, at the top
of a narrow staircase. You enjoyed
being contemporary with Charles.
That was part of you, as much
as the backache in the novitiate.

There were so many at the Profession
it was a matter of nods over heads,
and watching the damp rise up the servers' albs
on that wet day, under canvas, in the courtyard.
The blackberry picking and red polishing stone floors
were becoming things of the past.

We last met on the train going north.
It was hot and crowded;
you, in the unseasonal thick habit.
It was unsatisfactory again:
a matter of small talk, and I wondered
if it was the same for others,
where the knowing you well
was always yet to come.

Then the news in fragments:
your recent concern for fitness;
the shoes on the empty beach;
and day by day the certain possibility
of your being entirely out of reach.

The Orchard

Now we have apple trees
and a walled garden beyond the village.
Boys will come for the meagre, sour fruit
by way of the frames and the water butt.
It will be the heat of the day
they remember, when as old men
they make their mild confession
to the new incumbent. They will remember
the stalking through the undergrowth,
and the first sweat of guilt,
sweeter than the apple.
Eased out of a narrow pocket
it was worth only one tart bite
before an aimless chuck sent the birds
flying, and there was time to attend
to a graze and a pumping heart.

A Talk on William Byrd

The gas is turned on, but the old, soft
box of matches is not striking well enough.
The smell seeps through the iron shutters
from the kitchen into the Hall, thickening the air.
The few chairs for the talk on William Byrd
straddle the lines of the badminton court.
We face the back of the piano, beneath
a light bulb hanging like a plumb-line.
'This is the Ave Verum Corpus,' and the needle
is lowered into the second bar. Gas becomes incense.
Seagulls, like angels, glide through the aerials.

Bishop Taylor's Remedies against Tediousness of Spirit

I know the clergy around Llanfihangel
are sometimes out of sorts with the full
Morning and Evening Prayer, said each day.
My suggestion is that they sing
even alone in the church, what they always say.
It doesn't have to be Purcell
or Pelham Humphryes; anything
that touches the fancy will sound well
and return a relish to praying.

Parish Visit

Going about something quite different,
begging quiet entrance
with nothing in my bag, I land
on the other side of the red painted step
hoping things will take effect.
The space in the house is ten months old
and time has not yet filled it up,
nor is the headstone carved.
He died when he was twenty
and she was practised at drawing
him back from the brink
cajoling in spoons of soup.
We make little runs at understanding
as the winter afternoon
lights up the clothes on the rack;
we make so many
the glow in the grate almost
dips below the horizon,
but does not quite go out.
It is a timely hint
and I make for the door and the dark yard,
warmed by the tea,
talking about things quite different.

Scattering Ashes

The nose of the pick-up lifted
into the sky and then down onto the fell
as we made our way to the spot
he drove to himself to drop hay
in bad winters and as he got lame.
From where we stopped, we could see
the farm house and the tops of hills
which for a moment seemed to pour in
on the random heap of an old sheep pen.
Willy fed the ash out like a trail
of gunpowder. It blew among us
taking the words with it: ashes; sacred;
our brother here departed. We stood
fixed awkwardly as hawthorn trees watching
the white ashes of a man who once stamped
this ground, fly off in fancy with the wind.
Arms were wrapped like scarves round shoulders;
and the dog, whistled out of the back,
wove in front of the car a sad reel
as we followed the fresh tracks home
through all the open gates on the land.

David Scott was born in 1947 in Cambridge. He was brought up in the Midlands, and is now a parish priest in rural Cumbria. He won the *Sunday Times*/BBC national poetry competition in 1978. His publications include two pamphlets, *Thorn and Flower* (Dodman Press, 1976) and *Days Out* (Mandeville Press, 1978). *A Quiet Gathering* is his first book-length collection of poems.

David Scott has written four plays with Jeremy James Taylor for the Children's Music Theatre. *Captain Stirrick* was performed at the National Theatre in 1981; and *Bendigo Boswell*, a BBC commission, was televised last year. Their most recent play, *Powder Monkeys,* was commissioned for the 1984 Cambridge Festival.

He is married, and has a son and a daughter.

Graham Arnold is a member of the Brotherhood of Ruralists.